Introduction

From the creator of the ASO 2016 Learn App Store Optimization (extremely shrunk-down version was distributed for free, Amazon has the full version) and many other "black hat", "grey hat", and "white hat" posts, the general public can now have access to the most hidden ASO tactics. This book is purely educational. I strongly believe that in the new digital era, sharing of information will encourage collaboration which will eventually promote growth and the need of advancement. The establishment will also help app developers to become more aware of and understand what can be done in the digital world so they can make informed decisions on their apps. If you find this book useful, please help me by sharing it with your friends and colleagues.

Marlon Franco of Games Gadgets & Gizmos is an ASO hacker, a start-up, data analysis and urgency junkie who spends most of his time looking for ways to manipulate apps' rankings in the App Store. He's the owner of Games Gadgets & Gizmos, Skate Shoes PH, and Best Food In Town, who graduated with a degree in Information Technology in the Philippines.
It's not a secret that there are now a good number of ASO service providers all over the World. Marlon, the ASO Hacker is one of them. He is officially going 4 years and has grown to a team of 5 strong. Just for giving you some news on the services that he provides, here's what's been happening to him as an ASO service provider here in the Philippines.

Social Media

It's not that much but his persona has slowly but surely grown its social circle. He has seen increased in engagement on his Facebook Page and Twitter and has thousands of people subscribed to his Email List – all of whom we've kept confidential. They are happily receiving his latest entries every time he posts a new one.

Direct

He gets around 3,000 direct traffic to his blog entries each month. In the three plus years that he's blogging, He considers himself blessed to have that number recognize his branding. I think that branding has a lot to do with ASO today.

The point of the matter is, it's not an overnight thing to build a community and brand. It takes a lot of hard work, consistency, creativity, and commitment. These are just numbers. The underlying value of his company isn't really in how big our community is but how well he serves them and how well he takes care of his brand.

ASO Services

If you didn't know, he provides ASO services (duh!) around the World. He has catered to international and Philippine brands in his 2 official years in the ASO industry. He does more than just ASO, as he cares about his clients' brands. You can check out his ASO and Internet Marketing Packages here.
He recently revamped his ASO Services website and has published an ASO Book for dummies – check it out !

Acknowledgment and Dedications

My sincere thanks go first and foremost to my beloved wife, Mara Franco, who has been my inspiration and motivation for continuing to improve my knowledge in ASO and move my career forward. She is my rock, and I dedicate this book to her. I also thank my wonderful children: Marga & Teo, for always making me smile and for understanding on those weekend mornings when I was writing this ebook instead of playing games with them. I hope that one day they can read this book and understand why I spent so much time in front of my computer. I'd like to thank my parents, for allowing me to follow my ambitions throughout my childhood. My family, including my in-laws, have always supported me throughout my career and authoring this book and I really appreciate it. I look forward to discussing this book with my family at future gatherings as I'm sure they will all read it soon.

First of all, What Is ASO?

For the uninitiated, ASO stands for app store optimization and it refers to the practice of making your app available for app store search engines like Apple and Google to include in their results when someone submits a search. When you simply publish an app, these search stores will generally find it and include it in their massive index of apps. But you want to do more than getting indexed right? You want to make sure that these app stores associate your app with the keywords that your customers and potential customers are typing into the search field, hoping to find an app like yours.

OK, so what is Blackhat ASO?

BlackHat refers to aggressive App Store Optimization strategies that can or may violate the search App Store's guidelines and best practices.

The primary recognizable trait of blackhat app store optimization is its disregard for users and its primary focus on manipulating keyword app rankings.

Most common strategies include app traffic boost, downloads automation, and keyword stuffing. These are said to be proven to help position low-quality apps in the App Store search results.

Eventually, the App stores (iTunes and Google Play) caught on and tackled blackhat practices by updating their search algorithms. From then on, an app would be penalized by them when using black hat tactics.

However, there are still blackhat strategies that work (you'll learn more about it later on) and it will help you skyrocket your app's organic traffic.

In China, if you don't know what the slang word "shuabang" means, you are definite out of the loop. It is the hottest topic in the Chinese mobile marketing circle nowadays.

Shuabang is an ASO industry and considered one of the most troubling gangs of system gamers who specialized in providing Black Hat ASO services. Typically, they sell installs and user ratings to app developers to help boost their profile.

Shuabang Blackhat Methods for iOS

Shuabang practitioners have created millions of phantom Apple iTunes accounts

They offer new downloads, ratings or whatever measurements required to manipulate the numbers.

Shuabang is a sport, and it isn't a cheap one. Shuabang fees start at $1,500 to get into a top 100 list — a top 10 listing costs as much as $10,000 per day. Pretty expensive eh?

When you hire a service, the company hire and subcontract 150 to 200 agents who will log in to iTunes using the Shuabang company's millions of iTunes accounts to download and review the apps as often as is needed to fulfill your order.

If they failed to deliver — be it downloads, the desired ranking or the period over which the ranking is maintained — your money will be refunded. No questions asked.

Shuabang methods include: boosting ratings all at once in just a couple of hours, doing it on a Friday to maximize exposure during the weekends or spreading it out over a month, yanking ratings up whenever they slip.

Shuabang Blackhat Methods for Android

They create Widgets to automatically download apps in order to get higher rankings in Android app stores. Also, it's no secret that many Chinese Internet companies have been secretly installing apps, or misleading users to uninstall competing ones on users' PCs or, more recently, mobile Android devices without their knowledge.

They create thousands of "Shanzhai" apps, spinoffs or knockoffs. No matter how many users those knockoffs can get, they carry ads or have in-app paid offerings. To attract users, lots of knockoffs use pictures of sexy models as app icons or take various shady tactics to tricking users into downloading those apps.

They secretly side load Android apps into users' devices that have rats. One compromised Android device must be very busy at night downloading all kinds of apps, opening them, and then uninstall them before their masters wake up in the morning. Shady ops go so far as to make purchases with users' online banking accounts.

BlackHat ASO - The Dark Side of App Store Optimization

The dark side of ASO, when done correctly, can yield staggering results...in addition to a high risk of getting your app banned from all the App Stores. Some of these techniques include keyword spamming and boosting.

Manufacturing Link Popularity

Same with Blackhat SEO, link popularity techniques are aimed at improving your app's business. Mostly, this is done to destroy a competitor's brand.

NegativeApp Reviews

Some marketers use cheap Indian labor to spam negative reviews on apps. It is used to try to ruin the competitors brand.

Email Spam

Lots of high margin apps spam unknowing new app developers asking for review exchanges. Some people may also spam for a competitor to try to destroy their brand.

3 Way Link Trade

Some people set up review exchange sites and have you register to their site that does not really provide anything. In exchange, you waste your time reviewing their apps, expecting that they'll return the favor. Yeah, there may be some three way link trades that are legit, but many are not.

ASO Propaganda

One of the quietest forms of so-called "dark" ASO is rumor mongering. By creating an appearance of authenticity for a particular tactic or method, an ASO can influence lesser ASOs to pursue that tactic. This is especially effective on new or part-time ASOs. In a competitive world, such diversions can secure exclusive access to opportunities, and can be very lucrative.

Take for example public "ASO Guidelines" including such things as books at Amazon, blogs or websites, public forums, and wikis. By aggregating a community of self-proclaimed ASOs to contribute "expert content", one creates an appearance of authority. App marketers or ASO experts are anxious to discover new methods or hacks to manipulate the App Store rankings because it provides them with some external validation as "knowledgable ASOs", visible to the uninformed public. Consequently, that consuming public, including wanna-be ASOs, are deceived into believing that the tactics and methods so publically documented are accurate and complete.

In fact, the real competitive tactics are absent from such publications, due to the simple fact that public disclosure would promptly render them ineffective. The consuming public is blind to the inherent sampling bias of the wiki (no real ASO secrets, no real competitive advantages). In some extreme cases, ASOs may publish such public ASO documents for the "public good" only until they are content-rich and popular among the naive, at which point the owner can slap ads all over it and monetized that free content for personal gain. Professional ASOs are wise enough to always inspect disclaimers.

8 Thoroughly Explained "ASO" App Store Optimization Hacks that work in 2016

There are many articles online and info hubs that offer you all the very best advice on App Store Optimization, the icons, screenshots, the title, competitors, the right way to write an app description this, oh, blah blah fish paste!

In reality, we are all just looking for that hack, right? That "one button fixes it all" thing. The ASO hack that defies the need for you to be a rocket scientist. We want that gratification. While it may look as though I am defeating the ends of justice here, or that this witcher is revealing his dark magic, the fact is that these dirty little hacks are totally within your control. Totally.

So here it is, the low down dirty ASO hack guide:

1) Reverse Engineer Competitors' App Description

The internet is a place where you can learn from the mistakes and successes of others. Many people try to reinvent the wheel which is often a complete waste of time. Most online strategies carried out by successful ASO experts leave a trail. This means you can find a successful online ASO campaign and easily reverse engineer it.

Most successful apps have a good and well-crafted description. This results to a higher range of social signals that indicate that it's a success. A large number of positive comments and sharing on various social media platforms is a clear sign that your competitor's content strategy is working.

2) Drive Traffic Through Less Competitive ASO Keywords

The quality and relevance of your keywords to your app continues to be a huge factor in successful ASO or marketing campaigns. There are 2 ways to effectively do this in 2016 - you need to focus on long tail keywords and trending news and events in an industry or locality.

3) Long Tail ASO Keywords

It may not be possible to rank highly for shorter, more popular keywords in the app store search engines.

However, long tail keywords can bring you huge amounts of traffic when this strategy is implemented correctly. Simple ways I have achieved this in the past include using the right keyword tools - google play, google tools, Mobileaction, and Searchman. Long tail keywords give those with fewer resources an opportunity to get traffic larger competitors ignore. In most cases the traffic generated through a long tail keyword strategy is more targeted than high level, expensive keywords too.

4) Piggyback on the popularity of the latest News and Events in an Industry or Location

Working in an industry or niche which provides local, national or international updates on a regular basis gives an app owner an opportunity to rank highly for popular keywords. By using the keywords found on news, trend or event, it's possible to piggyback on the popularity of the latest news, trends and events associated with your app.

This results in traffic competitors may not have considered.

5) Use Images and Video More Effectively

The popularity of images (icons and screenshots) and promotion video will continue to increase. These formats should be used to pre-sell apps in the coming year. Encouraging more likes, shares, tweets, pins and other sharing activities will be essential as more people realize how powerful these videos and images are.

More competition will exist online this year. However, using the hacks and information I've described above has the potential to improve the ASO activities of businesses and online marketers who wish to increase app traffic in the next twelve months.

6) Collaborating with clients more to leverage digital PR opportunities

An ASO strategy that we've been developing and implementing more and more at Games Gadgets & Gizmos is collaborating with our clients more to leverage digital PR opportunities. Folks in ASO have been talking about the similarities between PR and ASO for some time now (indeed did I, several years back), but not all understand how to think like PRs do and how to spot (or generate!) opportunities for press attention. Some of the most valuable links you can get are from mainstream media and news websites – these links are great for ASO as well as referral traffic, brand awareness and trust signals. 'PR' is great because it can mean a number of different things, at least one of which will be right for your business;

- News flow
- Interviews
- Internal customer data
- Surveys
- Industry press
- Media requests
- Linkbait
- Newsjacking
- And so much more

Whether starting small with small time bloggers, locally, industry or niche publications, or going in for a big fish in trying to make national and international news, PR is a great way of acquiring valuable, trusted and relevant links.

Whatever your strategy or approach, my recommendation would be to try and push the boundaries of creativity, to make your angle as hookable as possible – there are many other PRs and ASO experts doing the same thing all day, every day, so your ideas need to be creative, have a hook and be able to cut through the noise. Don't make your users happy, make them ecstatic; don't make them angry, make them furious; don't make them smile, make them belly laugh!

7) Ego Baiting is a very simple, fast and easy to execute ASO strategy

Ego baiting, as the name suggests is to boost the ego of an app owner with the intention of receiving a backlink in the process. This can be accomplished by simply composing a Top 10 or Top 20 or even Top 50 ASO experts or top apps blog. Ego Baiting is a very simple, fast and easy to execute ASO strategy that will allow any app in any niche to gain links from important, authoritative and relevant sites or social media outlets within the same industry.

Simply write about the top 10 apps this 2016 or top ASO experts and rank them in order of brilliance. Include a link if you wish to each blog, publish the post and then send an email to each app owners or ASO experts to let them know of your post so that they can stroke their own ego levels and share a link to the post on their app and social media profiles.

You can take this approach a bit further if you wish by making your post into an awards celebration and physically sending each app owners or ASO experts a reasonably priced award in the post. The backlinks will follow and these relevant authoritative links will give you a gradual rise in organic search traffic that will just keep rising and rising in the long run.

8) Focus on long tail keywords that converted!

It's a simple concept, but most often overlooked: build your strategies around long-tail, no volume ASO keywords that you know have converted, instead of building strategies based solely on keywords with the most search volume.

How to do it (part 1): There are two approaches you can take. First – do you have any historical data prior to (not provided)?

For one of my clients, we had been creating an ASO strategy around their highest volume target terms and it drove traffic, but none of it converted (fail!).

So, we flipped our strategy, and instead pulled a years' worth of data only on the organic keywords that actually resulted in a conversion and created content based only on these terms.

We did this despite the fact that these terms showed no monthly search volume (according to MobileAction) and drove only a handful of sessions each month.

The result: The new ASO strategy we developed and implemented brought in a little traffic, but nearly all of it converted!

How to do it (part 2): What about 2016 when you don't have organic keyword data from Apple and Google anymore?!

Of the keywords we found that converted for our clients, they all had these similar traits:

They were very long tail: containing at least 5 to 7 words within the search query

They were this long because they were often intention-based and semantic searches (e.g. someone speaking their query into a mobile device 'how to do…, where do I…, best place to…', etc.)

Because visitors were searching for such complex terms, they were often further along in the conversion funnel and as a result, more likely to convert!

Although Apple and Google claim that these terms have no volume and you can find these high value no volume target keywords for your own app by doing the following:

Export your queries report
Use the LEN function in Excel and pull the character count for each query
Narrow down to only search queries made up of at least 20 characters or more
Organize this narrowed list from A-Z to find common themes (for example: how do I..., where do I..., I want to..., etc.)

Then – develop your ASO strategy around these themes!
HAVE NO FEAR! Even though most of these terms will show little to no search volume in MobileAction, they are potentially likely to bring in at least some traffic that will have a much higher intention of converting. Enjoy having less traffic, but more conversions and more money!

App Store Optimization Hack - ASO Keyword Booster (iOS Only)

Hi everyone–this is me again. Today, I am going to tell you about a new ASO hack I'm really excited about - the ASO Keyword Booster.

For the uninitiated, ASO stands for app store optimization and it refers to the practice of making your app available for app store search engines like Apple and Google to include in their results when someone submits a search. When you simply publish an app, these search stores will generally find it and include it in their massive index of apps. But you want to do more than getting indexed right? You want to make sure that these app stores associate your app with the keywords that your customers and potential customers are typing into the search field, hoping to find an app like yours.

That's where our ASO Keyword Booster comes in. It helps you boost your keyword rankings for your app and will help you get the highest quality traffic. I'm so excited about this because I've spent a lot of my career helping app owners and developers deploy these practices on their apps to bring in more high-quality traffic, so I'm passionate about bringing this to you guys!

How ASO Keyword Booster Works

1. It's very simple, basically, you just need to select a keyword that you want to improve its ranking. You can do this by using Sensortower. A free account will do. Just add your app, go to App Store Optimization>keyword rankings, and select a keyword that you want to promote.

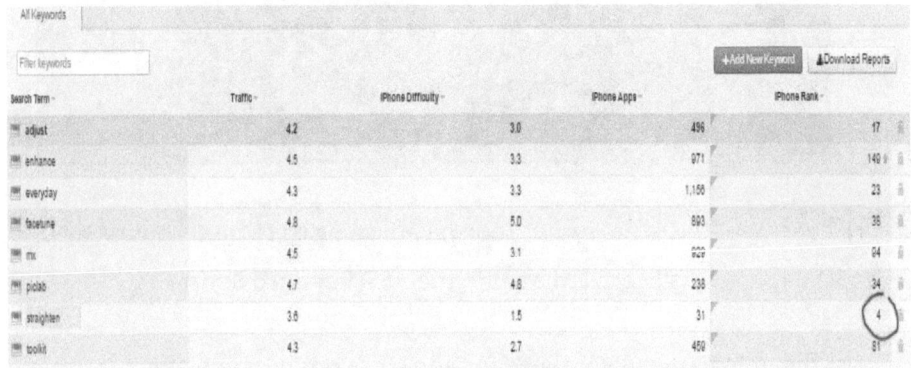

In this case, we use PicLab Toolkit MX as our example app and straighten as our main keyword.

2. What we'll do next is to open iTunes (if you don't have it installed yet, you can download it here). You need iTunes accounts because we need to download the app using the keyword that we want to promote (straighten). Don't worry, a few downloads per day can increase its ranking. If you want iTunes accounts that you can use, email me at admin@gamesgadgetsgizmos.info. It's not for free, though. I am selling it

for $1/account. Anyway, we need to download the app at least 20x a day to boost its ranking. Again, we need to use the keyword "straighten" to locate the app, and download it.

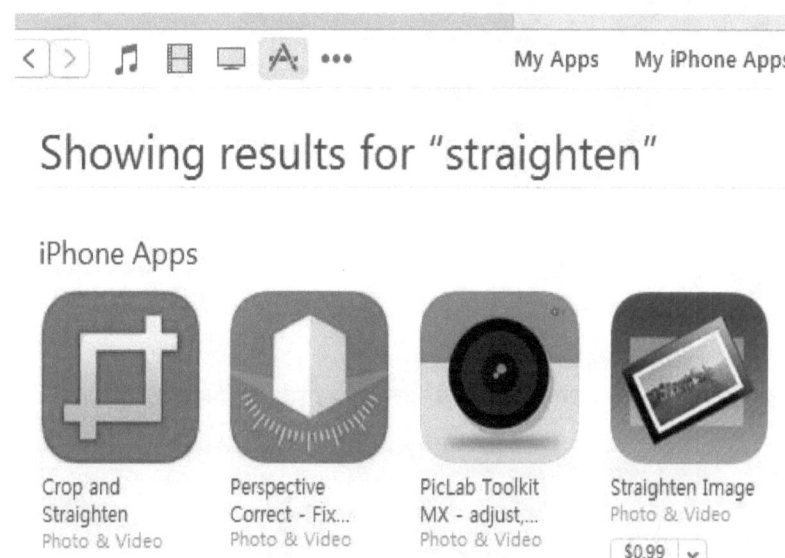

3. You may download the app as much as you can, on a daily basis - don't worry this hack is safe. Your app's keyword ranking will soon improve after a couple of downloads/days. See below:

Showing results for "straighten"

iPhone Apps

Crop and
Straighten
Photo & Video

`+ Get ⌄`

PicLab Toolkit
MX - adjust,...
Photo & Video

`Get ⌄`

Perspective
Correct - Fix...
Photo & Video

`+ $2.99 ⌄`

Straighten Image
Photo & Video

`$0.99 ⌄`

By the way, I also did the same on the keyword "wrinkles."

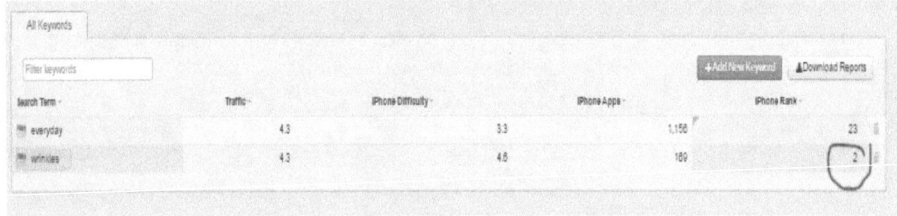

Search Term	Traffic	iPhone Difficulty	iPhone Apps	iPhone Rank
everyday	4.3	3.3	1,156	23
wrinkles	4.3	4.6	169	2

Showing results for "wrinkles"

iPhone Apps

Men's Facial
Fitness. Beauty...
Health & Fitness

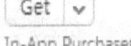
In-App Purchases

PicLab Toolkit
MX - adjust,...
Photo & Video

Download. ⌄

Oldify
Entertainment

$0.99 ⌄
In-App Purchases

Beauty Massage
Points - Smoot...
Health & Fitness

⁺ Get ⌄

Note: Results may vary, and of course your competitors will fight back. For sure, the Perspective Correct app owner will be pissed and will implement his/her own ASO strategy to reclaim its ranking.

ASO Keyword Booster FAQs

Is it Safe?

Yes, totally safe.

Real Accounts?

Yes, these are 100% real accounts. In fact, it has been 100% safe and tested on the developer account I have been using for this for over 6 months.

How long will I be on top?

Depends on how many downloads you will invest - the more the better.

iPhone or iPad?

You choose. Works in both.

App Store Optimization Hack - Maximize Your Free Sensortower Account

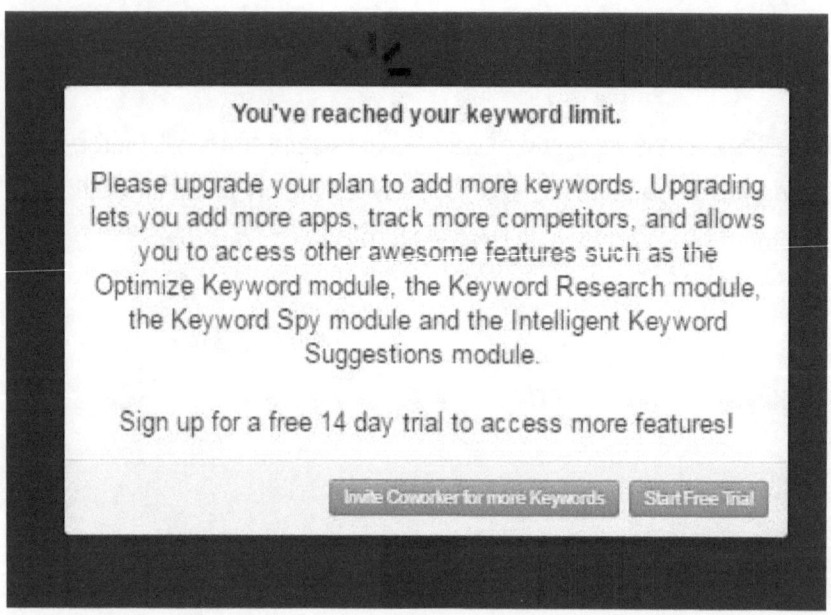

A higher App Store ranking for your chosen keywords makes it easier for people to find your app. In turn, this brings you more downloads.

Today, I am going to show you how can a free Sensor Tower account help you find the best keywords for your app.

How To Use Sensor Tower (Free Account) for Selecting Keywords

One of Sensor Tower's valuable features is the App Store Optimization section. It's designed to help users target a strong set of keywords.

With only 100 characters available for the keywords field in the App Store, each character counts. Sensor Tower can provide technical recommendations to prevent you needlessly chasing unnecessary keywords — for example, keywords in your app's title, or plural variations of keywords you already target.

It will also tell you if you have characters free to include more keywords, allowing you to make the most of what you have available. Moreover, it will even recommend keywords you should target, and provide some suggestions that you might not have considered.

However, Sensortower's starting price of $79 per month is not to be sneezed at, but if you're really looking for a highly effective tool to help with your App Store optimization, then it's well worth the investment.

But if you're budget is tight, and you're still in the process of building your profile as an ASO consultant, then this might help you.

If your Sensortower account is free, there's a limit on the number of keywords that you can search for rankings (8 keywords per day I think). But I have found a trick. I used to check keyword rankings in the Keyword Rankings section, but not anymore. You only need to use this feature when you already launched your app, and you need to know how well you ranked on the keywords that you have chosen.

But if you are still in the keyword researching phase, you can check your keywords using the Keyword Optimization section. Why? You can copy and paste as many as keywords you want in the keywords field and it will provide the same results. See the picture below.

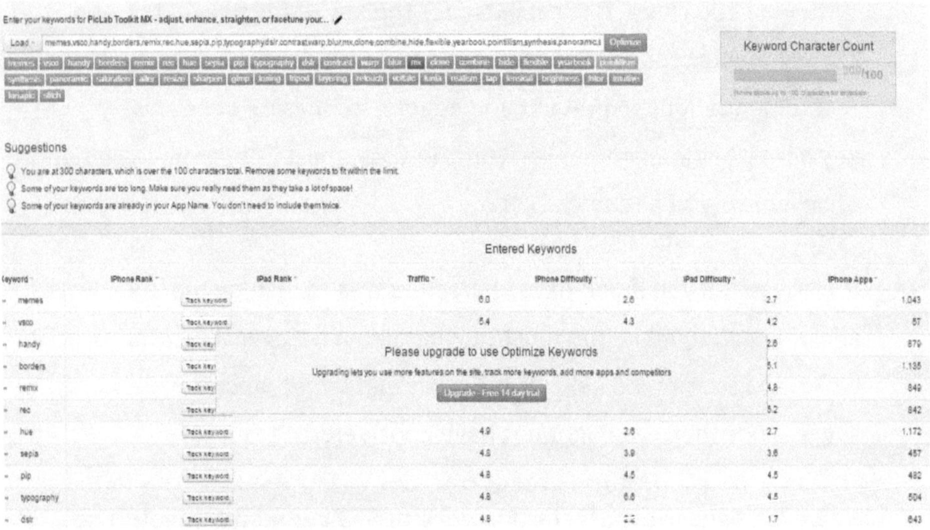

Then, you can select your best keywords. What I do is I select those with low-medium competition, and good ranking score. I also take into consideration the number of apps using the keyword. If it's more than 1,500, I ditch them.

Then, I'll highlight the keywords, CTRL+C

Paste it into a spreadsheet.

A	B	C	D	E	F	G	H
	iPhone	iPad		iPhone	iPad	iPhone	iPad
Keyword	Rank	Rank	Traffic	Difficulty	Difficulty	Apps	Apps
memes	Track keyword		6	2.6	2.7	1,043	680
vsco	Track keyword		5.4	4.3	4.2	57	35
handy	Track keyword		5.3	3.2	2.6	879	507
borders	Track keyword		5.2	4.4	5.1	1,135	797
remix	Track keyword		5.1	3.4	4.8	849	625
rec	Track keyword		5.1	4.4	5.2	842	540
hue	Track keyword		4.9	2.6	2.7	1,172	981
sepia	Track keyword		4.8	3.9	3.6	457	271
pip	Track keyword		4.8	4.5	4.5	482	408
typograph	Track keyword		4.8	6.6	4.5	504	354
dslr	Track keyword		4.8	2.2	1.7	643	491
contrast	Track keyword		4.7	4.1	3.3	373	311
warp	Track keyword		4.7	4.7	3.1	456	337
blur	Track keyword		4.6	5.5	5.3	1,720	1,204
mx	Track keyword		4.5	3.1	3.5	929	682
clone	Track keyword		4.4	5.6	3.9	622	461
combine	Track keyword		4.7	5.4	5.2	1,082	847
hide	Track keyword		4.3	6	5.1	2,025	2,256
flexible	Track keyword		4.7	1.6	1.3	567	441
yearbook	Track keyword		4.6	2.1	2.3	103	103
pointillism	Track keyword		4.5	2.7	2.5	18	17
synthesis	Track keyword		4.5	0.9	1	293	250
panoramic	Track keyword		4.4	3.9	3.6	230	172
saturation	Track keyword		4.3	3.4	5.2	224	168
alter	Track keyword		5	6.5	3.7	243	133

Delete Columns B and C

Keyword	iPhone Rank	iPad Rank	Traffic	iPhone Difficulty	iPad Difficulty	iPhone Apps	iPad Apps
memes	Track keyword		6	2.6	2.7	1,043	680
vsco	Track keyword		5.4	4.3	4.2	57	35
handy	Track keyword		5.3	3.2	2.6	879	507
borders	Track keyword		5.2	4.4	5.1	1,135	797
remix	Track keyword		5.1	3.4	4.8	849	625
rec	Track keyword		5.1	4.4	5.2	842	540
hue	Track keyword		4.9	2.6	2.7	1,172	981
sepia	Track keyword		4.8	3.9	3.6	457	271
pip	Track keyword		4.8	4.5	4.5	482	408
typograph	Track keyword		4.8	6.6	4.5	504	354
dslr	Track keyword		4.8	2.2	1.7	643	491
contrast	Track keyword		4.7	4.1	3.3	373	311
warp	Track keyword		4.7	4.7	3.1	456	337
blur	Track keyword		4.6	5.5	5.3	1,720	1,204
mx	Track keyword		4.5	3.1	3.5	929	682
clone	Track keyword		4.4	5.6	3.9	622	461
combine	Track keyword		4.7	5.4	5.2	1,082	847
hide	Track keyword		4.3	6	5.1	2,025	2,256
flexible	Track keyword		4.7	1.6	1.3	567	441
yearbook	Track keyword		4.6	2.1	2.3	103	103
pointillism	Track keyword		4.5	2.7	2.5	18	17
synthesis	Track keyword		4.5	0.9	1	293	250
panoramic	Track keyword		4.4	3.9	3.6	230	172
saturation	Track keyword		4.3	3.4	5.2	224	168
alter	Track keyword		5	6.5	3.7	243	133

And you now have a good looking keyword research report.

	A	B	C	D	E	F
	Keyword	Traffic	iPhone Difficulty	iPad Difficulty	iPhone Apps	iPad Apps
	pointillism	4.5	2.7	2.5	18	17
	vsco	5.4	4.3	4.2	57	35
	yearbook	4.6	2.1	2.3	103	103
	saturation	4.3	3.4	5.2	224	168
	panoramic	4.4	3.9	3.6	230	172
	alter	5	6.5	3.7	243	133
	synthesis	4.5	0.9	1	293	250
	contrast	4.7	4.1	3.3	373	311
	warp	4.7	4.7	3.1	456	337
	sepia	4.8	3.9	3.6	457	271
	pip	4.8	4.5	4.5	482	408
	typograph	4.8	6.6	4.5	504	354
	flexible	4.7	1.6	1.3	567	441
	clone	4.4	5.6	3.9	622	461
	dslr	4.8	2.2	1.7	643	491
	rec	5.1	4.4	5.2	842	540
	remix	5.1	3.4	4.8	849	625
	handy	5.3	3.2	2.6	879	507
	mx	4.5	3.1	3.5	929	682
	memes	6	2.6	2.7	1,043	680
	combine	4.7	5.4	5.2	1,082	847
	borders	5.2	4.4	5.1	1,135	797
	hue	4.9	2.6	2.7	1,172	981
	blur	4.6	5.5	5.3	1,720	1,204

Next is I select all my keywords

1	Keyword	Traffic	Difficulty	Difficulty	Apps	Apps
2	pointillism	4.5	2.7	2.5	18	17
3	vsco	5.4	4.3	4.2	57	35
4	yearbook	4.6	2.1	2.3	103	103
5	saturation	4.3	3.4	5.2	224	168
6	panoramic	4.4	3.9	3.6	230	172
7	alter	5	6.5	3.7	243	133
8	synthesis	4.5	0.9	1	293	250
9	contrast	4.7	4.1	3.3	373	311
10	warp	4.7	4.7	3.1	456	337
11	sepia	4.8	3.9	3.6	457	271
12	pip	4.8	4.5	4.5	482	408
13	typograph	4.8	6.6	4.5	504	354
14	flexible	4.7	1.6	1.3	567	441
15	clone	4.4	5.6	3.9	622	461
16	dslr	4.8	2.2	1.7	643	491
17	rec	5.1	4.4	5.2	842	540
18	remix	5.1	3.4	4.8	849	625
19	handy	5.3	3.2	2.6	879	507
20	mx	4.5	3.1	3.5	929	682
21	memes	6	2.6	2.7	1,043	680
22	combine	4.7	5.4	5.2	1,082	847
23	borders	5.2	4.4	5.1	1,135	797
24	hue	4.9	2.6	2.7	1,172	981
25	blur	4.6	5.5	5.3	1,720	1,204
26	hide	4.3	6	5.1	2.025	2.256

Copy paste it in a Word Document

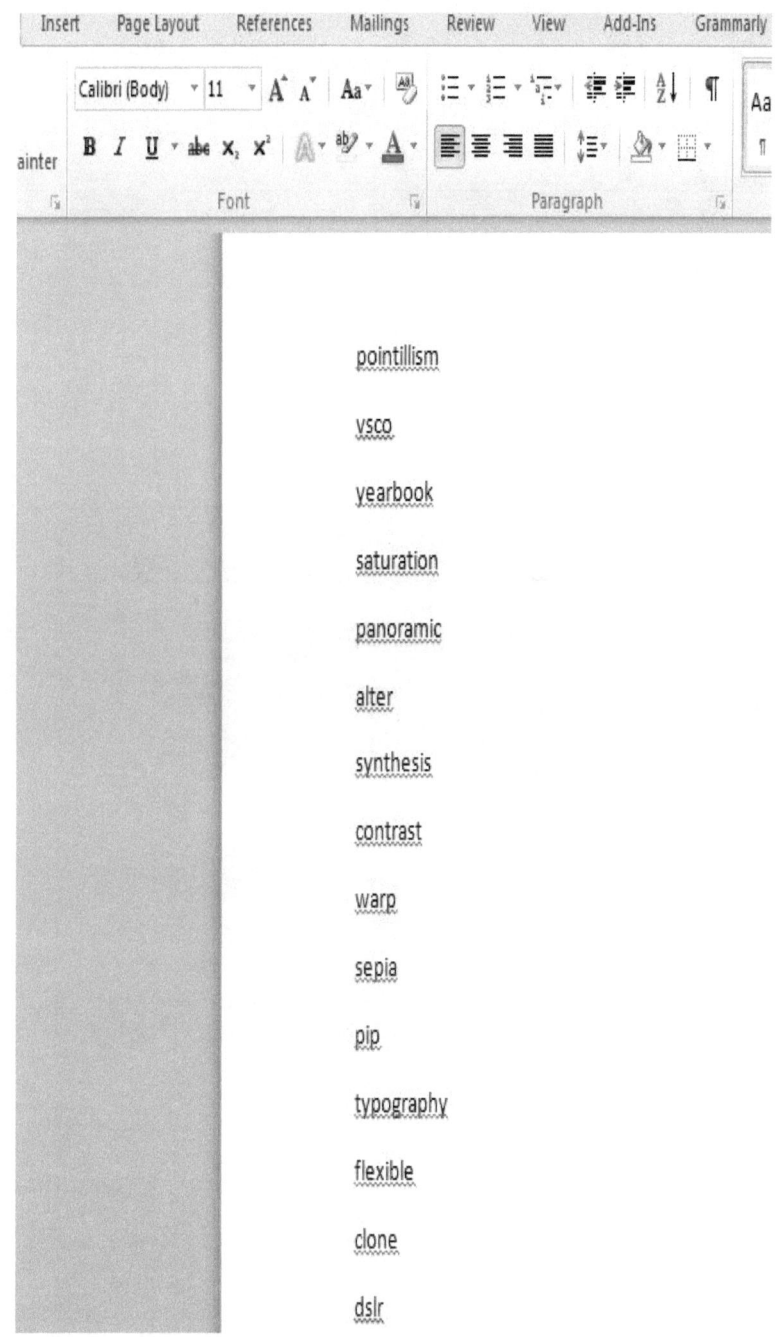

Insert   Page Layout   References   Mailings   Review   View   Add-Ins   Grammarly

Calibri (Body)   11   A A   Aa

ainter   B I U ▾ abe x₂ x²

Font   Paragraph

pointillism

vsco

yearbook

saturation

panoramic

alter

synthesis

contrast

warp

sepia

pip

typography

flexible

clone

dslr

Press CTRL+H, to find and replace (^p with ,) - this will show your keywords in the following format: keyword1,keyword2,keyword3,....

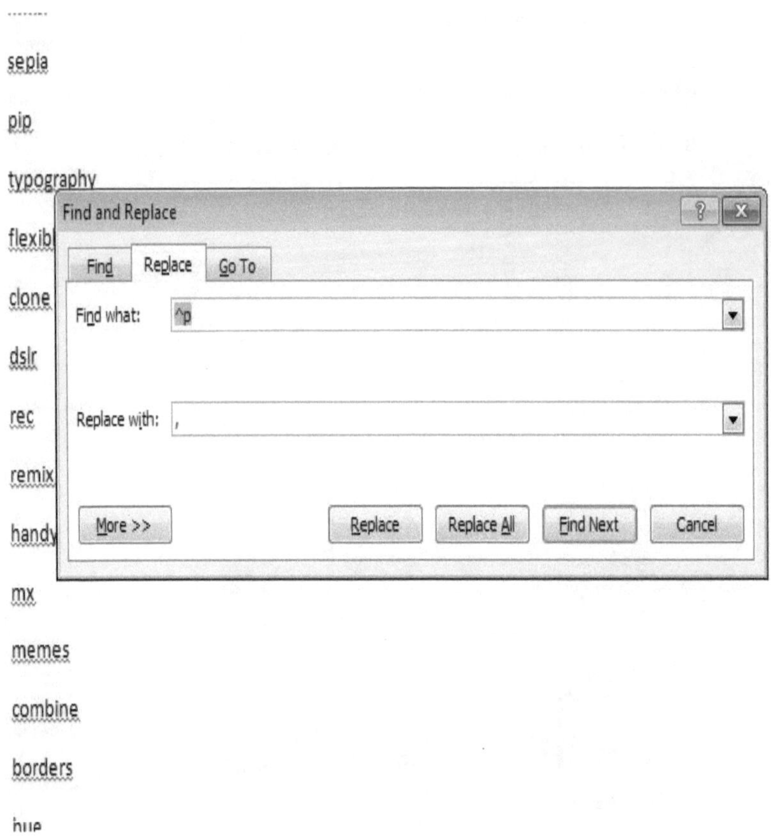

....

sepia

pip

typography

flexibl

clone

dslr

rec

remix

handy

mx

memes

combine

borders

hue

Find and Replace ? ✕

Find | Replace | Go To

Find what: ^p

Replace with: ,

[More >>] [Replace] [Replace All] [Find Next] [Cancel]

End Result:

pointillism, vsco, yearbook, saturation, panoramic, alter, synthesis, contrast, warp, sepia, pip, typography, flexible, clone, dslr, rec, remix, handy, mx, memes, combine, borders, hue, blur, hide|

I can now copy and paste these keywords in the Character Count Online textbox so I'll get 100 characters keywords set for US, SP (Spain), if it's more than 200, I can add a localization for CA-EN, Australia, or the UK. Cool eh?

I hope that these somewhat outlandish ASO tips have provided some useful insights and provided you as a reader with something to think about afterwards. . If you've had other cool tips or hacks in using Sensor Tower, I'd love to hear from you in the comments section below. Similarly, if you prefer a different App Store Optimization tool, let me know which one and why you think it's the better choice!